Nature's Wonders

THE GREAT BARRIER REEF

PATRICIA K. KUMMER

 **Marshall Cavendish**
Benchmark
New York

Marshall Cavendish Benchmark
99 White Plains Road
Tarrytown, NY 10591-5502
www.marshallcavendish.us

Expert Reader: Dr. Glenn R. Almany, ARC Centre of Excellence for Coral Reef Studies,
James Cook University, Townsville, Australia

All Internet addresses were correct and accurate at the time of printing.

Library of Congress Cataloging-in-Publication Data
Kummer, Patricia K.
The Great Barrier Reef / by Patricia K. Kummer
p. cm. — (Nature's Wonders)
Summary: "Provides comprehensive information on the geography, history, wildlife, peoples, and environmental
issues of the Great Barrier Reef"—Provided by publisher.
Includes bibliographical references and index.
ISBN 978-0-7614-2852-7
1. Coral reef biology—Australia—Great Barrier Reef (Qld.)—Juvenile literature. 2. Great Barrier Reef (Qld.)—
Juvenile literature. I. Title. II. Series.

QH197.K86 2008
578.77'8909943—dc22
2007026661

Editor: Christine Florie
Publisher: Michelle Bisson
Art Director: Anahid Hamparian
Series Designer: Kay Petronio

Photo research by Connie Gardner

Cover photo by Stephen Brink/Getty Images

The photographs in this book are used by permission and through the courtesy of: *Corbis:* Philip Spuryt/Stapleton
Collection, 1, 44, 47; Tom Van Sant, 8; Robert Yin, 14; Yann Arthus-Bertrand, 27; Lindsay Hebbard, 30; Brandon
D. Cole, 34; Pam Gardner, 43; Lowell Georgia, 48; Craig Lamotte, 66; Theo Allofs, 86, 89; Poodles Rock, 87; Bill
Varie, 88; *Alamy:* Mary Evans Picture Library, 51; *Minden Pictures:* Fred Bavendam, 3, 21; 37 (B); back cover, 40,
41, 68; Chris Newbert, 23; Georgette Douwma/npl, 37 (T); Flip Nicklin, 82; *Getty Images:* John W. Banaga, 5; Tim
Laman/National Geographic, 19; William J. Hebert, 24-25; Paul Chesley, 28-29; Herwarth Voigtman, 37(M); David
Torckler, 38; Hulton Archive, 50; Pete Atlunson, 70-71; AFP, 74, 80; Ezra Shaw, 77; Robert Nu/Minden Pictures,
79; *Dembinsky Photo Associates:* Jesse Cancelmo, 10; *The Image Works:* David Hall, 32, Mary Evans Picture Library, 53;
Digital Railroad: Stuart Westmorland, 13; *Photo Researchers:* L. Newman and A. Flowers, 17; Andrew J. Martinez, 20;
Bill Bachman, 63; *Danita Delimont:* Theo Allofs, 35; Jon Arnold Images, 61; *Peter Arnold:* Rodger Klein, 39.

Map (p. 6) and diagram (p. 18) by Mapping Specialists Limited

Printed in China

135642

CONTENTS

ONE

The Seventh Natural Wonder of the World

Coral reefs are everywhere. They are as close as the tropical aquariums in the nearest pet shop or in a friend's home. Some U.S. cities have huge aquariums with a special coral reef tank, such as the Shedd Aquarium in Chicago, Illinois. Of course, natural coral reefs are only found under warm, shallow sea and ocean waters. In the United States the largest coral reefs are off the eastern coast of Florida and among the Florida Keys, and along the Hawaiian Islands. More than 4,600 miles (7,400 kilometers) southwest of Hawaii, however, lies the world's largest area of coral reef—the Great Barrier Reef, the seventh natural wonder of the world.

WHERE IN THE WORLD IS THE GREAT BARRIER REEF?

The Great Barrier Reef is a part of the Indian-Pacific Ocean reef system that stretches from the Red Sea to the Coral Sea. To be more

◀ *An aerial view captures just a small section of the three thousand reefs that comprise Australia's Great Barrier Reef.*

MAP OF THE GREAT BARRIER REEF

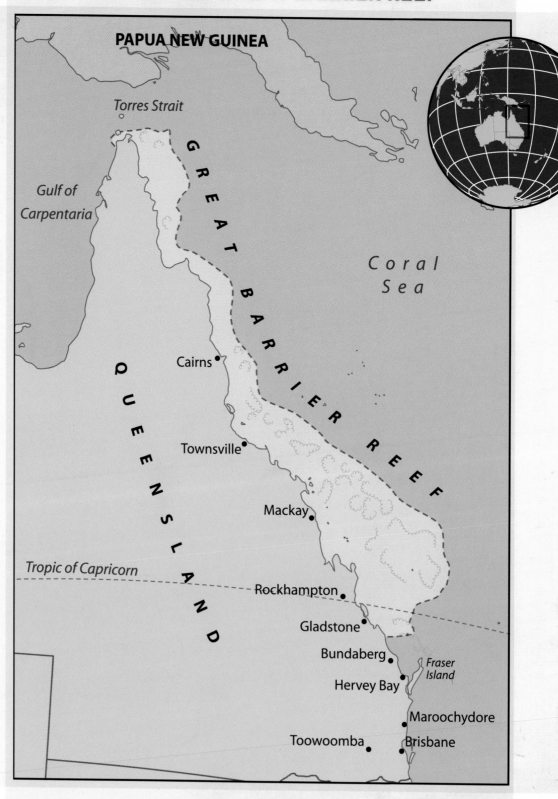

PAPUA NEW GUINEA

Torres Strait

Gulf of
Carpentaria

GREAT BARRIER REEF

Coral
Sea

QUEENSLAND

Cairns

Townsville

Mackay

Tropic of Capricorn

Rockhampton

Gladstone

Bundaberg

Fraser
Island

Hervey Bay

Maroochydore

Toowoomba

Brisbane

exact, the Great Barrier Reef juts up in the waters of the Coral Sea area of the South Pacific Ocean just off the northeast coast of Australia. That makes the Reef part of the Australian state of Queensland. Extending in length for 1,428 miles (2,300 km), the Reef reaches north into the Torres Strait—just south of Papua New Guinea—and south just below the Tropic of Capricorn.

All but the southern tip of the Great Barrier Reef lies between the Equator and the Tropic of Capricorn. Thus, the Reef is in the Tropic Zone—a hot, humid, and rainy climate zone with occasional fierce storms. The other part of the Tropic Zone lies north between the Equator and the Tropic of Cancer. Because coral reefs only grow in warm water with lots of sunshine, most of the world's coral reefs are found within the Tropic Zone. A few coral reefs lie just north or south of this zone.

WHAT IS THE GREAT BARRIER REEF?

The Great Barrier Reef is not one long continuous reef. Instead, it is a group of about three thousand reefs, which together form a **barrier reef**. A barrier reef is only one type of reef. Within the Great Barrier Reef, other kinds of coral reefs, such as **fringe reefs** and **platform reefs**, have also formed. This reef system of the Great Barrier Reef makes up about 20 percent of the world's coral reefs.

Like all other coral reefs, the reefs of the Great Barrier Reef system are alive. They are made up of billions of tiny animals called coral **polyps**, which continue to build the Reef each year. The Reef

Things to Remember about Being "Down Under"

Australia's nickname is "The Land Down Under" because that country and continent are south of, or "under," the Equator. Being south of, the Equator means that Australia (lower right on map) and the Great Barrier Reef are in the Southern Hemisphere. North America, Europe, and Asia are in the Northern Hemisphere.

In the Southern Hemisphere, many things occur just the opposite of the way they do in the Northern Hemisphere. For example, the seasons are different. When it is summer in the United States, Australia is having winter. When it is spring in Australia, leaves are falling in the United States. Also, going from north to south, the climate is different. In the United States, it is colder in the North and warmer in the South. In Australia and the Great Barrier Reef area, temperatures are warmer to the north and become cooler toward the south.

Australia ⎯⎯⎯

is also home to thousands of different species of fish and other marine life.

The Great Barrier Reef is a delicate world treasure. Its **ecosystem** of water, plants, animals, and humans must maintain a balance if it is to remain as the largest area of coral reef on earth. Because of the need for protection, the government of Australia created the Great Barrier Reef Marine Park in 1975. The park is managed by the Great Barrier Reef Marine Park Authority (GBRMPA), which regulates human activity on the Reef. In addition, in 1981, the United Nations Educational, Scientific, and Cultural Organization (UNESCO) named the Great Barrier Reef as a World Heritage Site. This status brought the Reef under the protection of the nations of the world. In 2004 the Australian government increased the area of the Great Barrier Reef Marine Park that is fully protected from fishing or other activities from 5 percent to around 33 percent.

AN UNUSUAL NATURAL WONDER

Most natural wonders are in isolated areas, far from highly populated cities, such as Uluru (Ayers Rock) in the middle of Australia or Ecuador's Galapagos Islands in the Pacific Ocean. Many natural wonders are best known for their beauty, such as those found in Yellowstone National Park, or for something unusual about their appearance, for example the formations in Utah's Monument Valley. Some of the world's natural wonders have the words *Great* or *Grand* as part of their names: the Great Barrier Reef, the Great Lakes, and

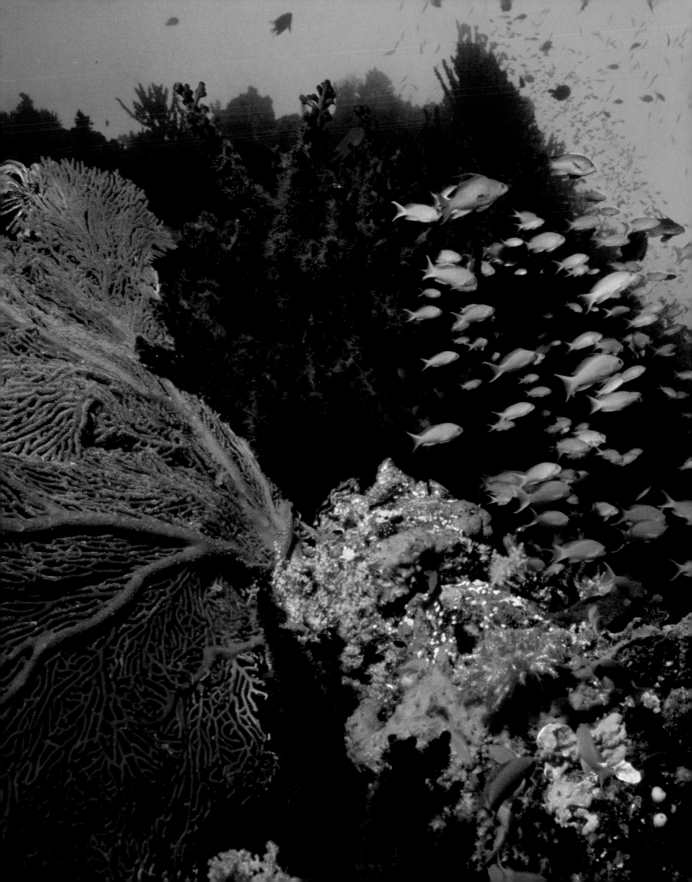

the Grand Canyon. The use of *great* and *grand* usually refers to an aspect of the wonder's physical dimensions, such as total area, depth, width, or length, which is true of the Great Barrier Reef. In fact, the size of the Great Barrier Reef makes it the only living thing on earth that is visible from outer space.

Although the Great Barrier Reef meets the usual natural wonder standards of great beauty and awesome size, it is an unusual natural wonder in many ways. First, the Reef is the only natural wonder of the world that is a living thing, changing and continuing to grow every year. Second, the Great Barrier Reef is the only natural wonder that is under water and as such provides a

◄ *The coral reefs and cays of the Great Barrier Reef provide homes for many plants and animals.*

home to a rich variety of marine life. Third, the Reef provides two useful services: it protects Queensland's coast from the rough waves of the Pacific Ocean, and it acts as a giant filter for the ocean. Fourth, the Reef provides recreational activities for more than 2 million people every year. Australians and visitors alike snorkel and dive around the Reef to experience firsthand the wonders of the Great Barrier Reef's underwater world.

Visitors to the Great Barrier Reef see firsthand ▸▸
an underwater, living, natural wonder.

TWO

Building the Reef

Today the three thousand reefs of the Great Barrier Reef cover 386,109 square miles (1 million sq. km) of Australia's northeastern **continental shelf** under the Coral Sea, extending through the Torres Strait almost to Papua New Guinea. This huge area is sometimes called the Great Barrier Reef Province. Its size is much bigger than the area included in the GBRMPA, which is 134,115 square miles (348,700 sq. km). In fact, the "Province" is an area more than half the size of the state of Alaska. There are eight other reef provinces in the Pacific Ocean.

In relation to the mainland of Queensland, the Reef is as close as a few miles offshore, such as at Daintree National Park in the north, or as much as 150 miles (240 km) from shore, at Mackay to the south. Between the mainland and the Reef lies a **lagoon** of calm, shallow water. Within the lagoon, 618 continental islands and about 350 coral **cays** (pronounced as kays or keys) add to the watery landscape.

◄ *Coral polyps are tiny live creatures that form a hard cuplike shell. These are orange cup polyps.*

How the Great Barrier Reef Came to Be

For millions of years, coral reefs have grown in warm, clear, tropical salt waters along continental shelves. Tiny animals called coral polyps are responsible for the continued building of these reefs, including those of the Great Barrier Reef. Coral polyps attach themselves to hard surfaces. At the birth of a new reef, the polyps attach themselves to the continental shelf or the sea floor. Scientists believe that this growth process has been going on for about 18 million years on the oldest parts of the Great Barrier Reef. They determined this by drilling deep into the Reef—as far as 1,640 feet (500 meters). That part of the Reef cannot be seen because it is buried beneath today's continental shelf and ocean floor. The oldest sections of the Reef are farthest to the north, where the warmest waters are.

The parts of the visible Reef that descend the deepest are thought to be about 500,000 years old. They date from the beginning of the last series of Ice Ages. When the last Ice Age began its decline about 18,000 years ago, the sea level rose as the ice melted. For about ten thousand years, the sea level rose and fell until it reached its present level about eight thousand years ago. When the sea level rose and the water warmed, reefs formed as coral polyps grew on hills that were now under water. When the sea level fell, the reefs were exposed and the coral died. The dead sections of the Reef are called fossil reefs. When the sea level rose again, the fossil reefs were covered by water and coral polyps returned and began rebuilding the reefs. This

The constant pounding of ▷▷
waves, as well as ocean winds,
shape the Great Barrier Reef.

process occurred over and over. Today the living sections of the Reef are estimated to be about eight thousand years old.

Although polyps build the Reef, wind and wave action shapes the Reef. The Great Barrier Reef has an outer edge/windward side and an inner edge/leeward side. The outer edge faces northeast into the Pacific Ocean's Coral Sea. Throughout the year, it is hit by strong waves created by winds blowing from the southeast. **Coral** that is less fragile is found on the outer edge exposed to waves. The inner edge of the Reef faces the lagoon and the mainland. Coral that is more fragile, such as staghorn and plates, is found on the inner edge.

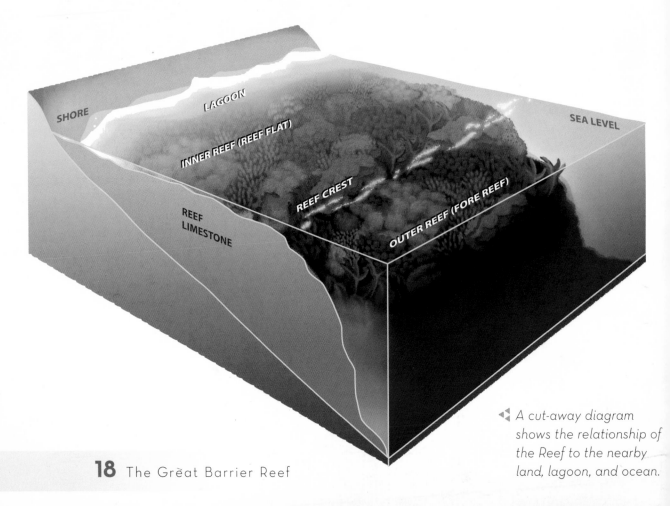

◄◄ A cut-away diagram shows the relationship of the Reef to the nearby land, lagoon, and ocean.

Sometimes, strong winds from cyclones or other storms blow out of the northwest. When that happens, coral on the inner edge is quickly and easily damaged. The wind tosses the coral on top of the reef, forming a boulder field.

POLYPS, ALGAE, AND LIMESTONE

The building process that began millions of years ago resulted in the huge limestone reefs that make up the Great Barrier Reef today. They were formed, and continue to be formed, by billions of individual coral polyps. Each polyp divides and multiplies in a process known

Coral polyps extend their feeding tubes to catch zooplankton as it floats by.

as budding, thus creating a colony of polyps. The polyps are tiny animals no bigger than a child's fingernail. Polyps have soft tubular bodies that look like flowers. The polyp's mouth is at the top of the tube and is surrounded by tentacles that reach out and collect food as it floats by. **Zooplankton**, an animal even smaller than polyps, is a favorite food. The polyps also filter calcium carbonate (dissolved limestone) from the sea water. The other end of the polyp's tubular body attaches itself to the Reef with secretions of the calcium carbonate. The calcium carbonate hardens into a cuplike shell, or

Star corals take on a greenish tint from the zooxanthellae that live inside them.

outer skeleton. As the polyp grows, so does its limestone skeleton. For protection, the polyp can contract into the shell. When the polyp dies, its hardened skeleton provides a place for new polyps to attach themselves.

Polyps receive help in producing their limestone shells. Single-celled **algae** plants, called **zooxanthellae** (pronounced zo-uh-zan-THE-lee), live within each polyp. The zooxanthellae and the polyps help each other in what is called a **symbiotic relationship**. Because zooxanthellae need sunlight, coral reefs grow close to the surface of the water so sunlight easily reaches the zooxanthellae. Like all plants, zooxanthellae produce nutrients using the sun's energy in a process called photosynthesis. Some of the nutrients produced by the zooxanthellae are used as food by the coral polyp. In fact, the polyp receives about 98 percent of its food from the zooxanthellae. The polyp also receive its tan, brown, or green color from the zooxanthellae.

Coral polyps reproduce in two ways: budding and spawning. In budding, a small growth, or bud, develops on the body of an adult polyp. When the bud is large enough, it separates from the adult. The new polyp begins to build its own limestone skeleton. Budding helps the colony and the reef grow.

A reef also increases in size through a mass spawning. This event takes place once a year on the Great Barrier Reef. About 135 of the Reef's four hundred **species** of coral take part in this mass spawning. In November, a few nights after the first full moon of summer, coral polyps release sperm and eggs. When the sperm and eggs meet, they form larvae that float away in the water. Many of the larvae are eaten

A staghorn coral colony releases eggs and sperm during the annual mass coral spawning.

by fish and other marine animals. However, some of them settle on hard surfaces far from their parents. Each new polyp immediately begins producing limestone, thus starting a new coral colony. Then, through budding, the polyp increases the size of an existing coral colony.

About four hundred different species of coral live on the Great Barrier Reef. All four hundred of them are found on the reefs in the warmer northern waters. Only about half of the species live in the cooler southern waters of the Reef. There are two types of coral: hard and soft. Hard corals—those with outer limestone skeletons—are the only ones that build reefs. Some hard coral colonies look like tables or shelves. Staghorn coral and brain coral are two common kinds of hard coral. Gorgonian, or soft, corals are also colonies of polyps, but their skeletons are on the inside. They come in many shapes and look like bushes, fans, fingers, and whips as they wave in the water. Hard and soft corals add much color to the Reef. They come in all shades of colors of the rainbow. The colors of some corals are so intense that they almost look artificial.

Hard and soft coral make up the ▷▷
four hundred types of coral on
the Great Barrier Reef.

The Sun and Moon Affect the Reef

Both the sun and the moon affect life on the Great Barrier Reef. The plants in the Reef's waters need sunlight to perform photosynthesis. It is through this process that plants make their food. They use energy from the sun to change water and carbon dioxide into food, and as a by-product plants give off oxygen into the water. The sun's rays can only reach to about 60 feet (18 m) below the water's surface. That is why plants, including zooxanthellae, grow at shallow depths. Because coral polyps depend on

zooxanthellae for 98 percent of their food, they, too, are found in shallow water.

The gravitational pull of the moon on the earth regulates the changing tides—the high and low water fluctuations of the oceans. At low tide (below), the moon pulls the tide, or water, out to sea, which results in wider beaches and exposure of the tops of coral reefs. High tide, on the other hand, occurs when the moon pulls the tide, or water, back toward land and over the reefs. This phenomenon of low tide/high tide takes place twice each day. With each tidal motion, the water of the Great Barrier Reef is stirred up, making more food available to the coral polyps and other marine life on the Reef.

Reefs and Cays

The Great Barrier Reef has three types of reefs: ribbon, platform, and fringe. Ribbon reefs are also known as barrier reefs. They run parallel to Queensland's coastline but are separated from the coast by lagoon waters. The ribbon reefs have long, thin, high limestone walls that act as barriers between the lagoon water and the open Coral Sea. The ribbon reefs are found only in the northern section of the Great Barrier Reef from Cooktown into the Torres Strait. Their windward or seaward side marks the outer edge of Australia's northeastern continental shelf. Channels deep enough for ships to use separate the individual ribbon reefs. Scientists have given most of the ribbon reefs identification numbers rather than names.

Platform reefs, also called patch reefs, are the most common type of reef in the Great Barrier Reef. This type of reef is found between the Australian coastline and the ribbon reefs. Cockburn Reef and Nomad Reef are good examples of northern platform reefs. Large groups of platform reefs, such as the Swain Reefs and the Pompey Reefs, are found in the southern part of the Reef system. Some platforms have grown as tall as 427 feet (130 m).

At various spots along the Great Barrier Reef system, more than 350 areas of land stand out. Although they look like islands, these pieces of land are coral cays. Coral cays are formed from the dead coral of platform reefs that grew too tall. The pounding of the ocean's waves grind the dead coral into sediment that looks like grains of sand. Throughout many years, the sediment builds up to form a coral

Fringe reefs, seen in the shallow water near Lizard Island, attach to the shore.

cay. Over time, seeds blown by the wind and dropped by birds take root and grow into grasses, trees, and other plants on the cays. These plants then provide places for birds to nest and to breed. Of the 350 cays, only 70 of them have names. Low Isles is a group of coral cays offshore from Port Douglas. Heron Island and Lady Elliot Island are famous cays in the southern part of the Reef.

Fringe reefs are attached to the shores of the Reef's islands and to some parts of Queensland's northern mainland. Great Keppel Island, the Whitsunday Islands, Hinchinbrook Island, Lizard Island, and Magnetic Island have especially large fringe reefs. Flat, disk-shaped coral colonies live on the inner or beach side of fringe reefs. The middle sections of fringe reefs have more plants (algae) than coral. However, a variety of coral grow on the outer (water) edges of fringe reefs.

Islands off the coast of Queensland offer miles of sandy beaches.

MAINLAND AND ISLANDS

The distance between the mainland of Australia and the Reef increases from north to south. In parts of the far north, the Daintree Rainforest extends beyond white sandy beaches and touches the Reef. The rain forest is more than 130 million years old and makes up part of UNESCO's Wet Tropics World Heritage Site. This is the only place in the world where two World Heritage Sites—the rain forest and the Reef—are found one next to another.

Much of Queensland's coastline is lined with wide, white sand beaches. Since the mid-1800s, growth and development of those

areas has meant that some beaches have become the front yards of towns and cities along the coast. Other areas of the coast, especially to the north, have large forests of mangrove trees. These trees grow where warm salt water from the lagoon meets and mixes with freshwater from the land. The freshwater comes from rivers and from rainwater that runs off the land.

In the lagoon, between the mainland and the Reef, lie about six hundred continental islands. These islands were formed about ten thousand years ago when the ice from the last Ice Age melted. Water from the melted ice flooded the lowlands along the coast of Australia.

The Whitsunday Islands are the largest group of islands in the Great Barrier Reef.

Land that was not flooded remained above water as islands. Because they were originally part of the continent of Australia, today they are called continental islands.

About 250 of the continental islands have names. Great Keppel Island is a large island with wide beaches in the southern part of the lagoon. Farther north, near the middle of the Great Barrier Reef, is the Whitsunday Island group, made up of seventy-four islands. Fringe reefs have formed along most of the Whitsunday Islands. Good-sized islands still farther north include Hinchinbrook, Dunk, Fitzroy, and Lizard islands. Lizard Island is covered by high mountains but also has many wide sandy beaches that are fringed with coral reefs.

CLIMATE

A warm, wet climate is needed for a healthy coral reef system. Obviously, the "wet" is provided by the seawater. The warmth is provided by the sun. Water temperatures on the Reef range from 66 degrees Fahrenheit (19 degrees Celsius) in the coldest winter month of July to 82 °F (28 °C) in the warmest summer month of February. Air temperatures over the Reef range from 81 °F (27 °C) in July to 91 °F (34 °C) in February.

Instead of a four-season year, the Reef area and mainland experience two seasons: a wet summer season and a dry winter season. The dry season lasts from May to October, and the wet season extends from November to April. During the wet period, the Reef and the mainland from Rockhampton to the Cape York Peninsula experience hot, humid weather. The wettest months are January, February, and March. Each month, rainfall ranges from 7 inches (18 centimeters) in Rockhampton, to 14 inches (36 cm) in Mackay and Townsville, to 21 inches (53 cm) on the Cape York Peninsula.

The wet season is also the time when tropical storms called cyclones blow through northeastern Queensland and the Reef. In the United States these windstorms are called hurricanes. The cyclones that hit Queensland and the Reef develop in the Indian Ocean and blow out of the northwest. They usually cross the Cape York Peninsula between Cooktown and Townsville and then continue out over the Great Barrier Reef. The cyclones' strong winds create huge waves that crash onto the reefs, damaging the coral.

On March 19 and 20, 2006, Cyclone Larry blew through with 180-mile- (290-km-) per-hour winds. It flattened banana and sugarcane crops on the mainland and destroyed the northwestern coasts of some islands. Of the reefs, Feather, Ellison, and Taylor were the most heavily damaged. On some reefs, as much as 30 percent of the coral was broken. Cyclones have been hitting the Reef for thousands of years, however, and the coral bounces back quickly.

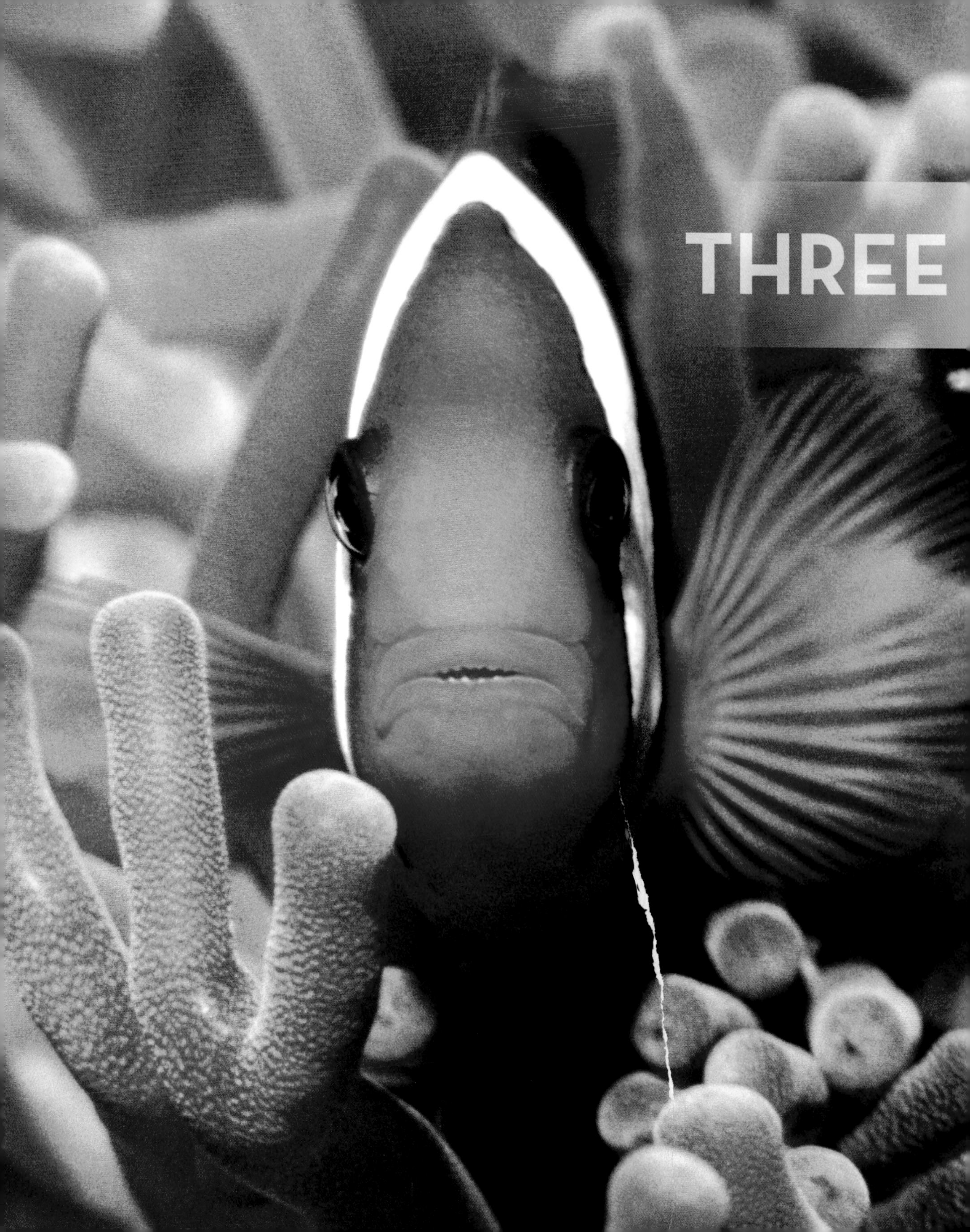

THREE

Life on the Reef

The Great Barrier Reef teems with life. In fact, coral reefs are the richest marine habitat on earth. Only rain forests on land have a larger variety of species, and coral reefs are sometimes called the rain forests of the sea. Besides the four hundred varieties of coral themselves and the algae that live in the coral polyps, the Reef provides a home to more than 1,500 species of fish, more than 5,000 species of mollusks, 6 kinds of turtles, and many other varieties of marine animal and plant life. In addition to the underwater life of the Reef, 215 species of birds have permanent or temporary homes on nearby cays and islands. What is even more amazing is that new species of Reef plants and animals are still being discovered.

PLANTS OF THE REEF AND NEARBY LAND

The simplest plants—single-celled algae—are plentiful in the Reef's waters and come in many colors. In all, about 450 species of algae are part of the Reef. Many of the Reef's fish and other marine life rely on algae as a part of their diet. Green algae, known as *Halimeda*,

◀ *Marine life is found in abundance on the Reef. Here, a clownfish hides in a sea anemone.*

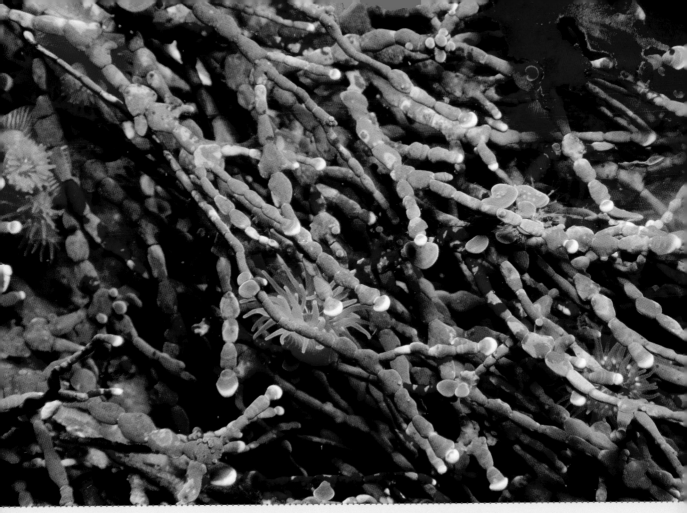

Coralline red algae have a stiff and rigid appearance. They are the most common form of marine algae.

grow in large beds on the floor of the Reef. These beds are the world's largest areas of *Halimeda*. Two kinds of algae help build the Reef. Zooxanthellae live within the coral polyps and help the polyps secrete limestone that becomes a part of the Reef. The colors of the zooxanthellae algae range from green to yellow to brown. Coralline red algae grow and secrete limestone between pieces of coral, thus helping to bind the Reef together. Two types of these coralline red algae—*Lithothamnion* and *Porolithon*—form a crust on the Reef's rims. The reddish purple color of the rims has become one of the Reef's well-known characteristics.

Growing in the sands of the continental shelf are large pastures of sea grass. Fifteen species of these grasses grow in Reef and coastal waters. Dugongs, also known as sea cows, graze on the sea grass. About 15 percent of the world's dugongs live on the Reef. The sea grasses are also an important source of food for the Reef's turtle population.

Lagoon waters on Queensland's coast support mangrove trees. At least thirty-seven different species of mangroves are found in those areas. Some of each mangrove's root system is exposed above ground. When the tide is out, the roots look like a tangle of legs. For that reason, mangroves are sometimes called walking trees. The tangled roots provide a sheltered place for the juveniles of many species of the Reef's fish and shellfish. The mangroves'

During low tide, the roots of these mangroves are visible at the Daintree National Park in Queensland.

roots also filter nitrogen and phosphorus from water that runs from the mainland into the lagoon. This filtering process helps keep the Reef's waters crystal clear.

Ancient Mangrove Forests

In 2005 scientists from the Australian Institute of Marine Science discovered nine-thousand-year-old mangroves buried 27 inches (70 cm) beneath the Great Barrier Reef. Some of the trees still had branches and leaves on them. This discovery shows that the rise of sea level at the end of the last Ice Age was about twenty times faster than originally thought. From their findings, the scientists believe that such a fast rise could occur again. If it did, great damage would take place along coastal areas around the world.

About 2,200 other plant species are also found on the continental islands. Eucalyptus trees cover the hilly Whitsunday Islands. Hoop pines, which are up to four hundred years old, are also found on those islands.

A WORLD OF UNUSUAL FISH

Rivaling the coral for flash and color are the Reef's two thousand species of fish. The colors and patterns of the fish act as camouflage as they weave among the coral or slip into crevices in the Reef. Some fish, such as blennies, gobies, and sea horses, are hard to see because they blend in with their surroundings. Sometimes a fish's bright color, such as the orange-red color of the firefish, warns other fish not to try to eat it—the deep color might mean, "I'm poisonous, so don't eat me."

Besides color and camouflage, the Reef's fish have other ways of protecting themselves. Each night the greensnout parrotfish makes a mucous sac around itself before bedding down. In this way, predators—other animals that would like to eat them—cannot smell the parrotfish. The fins of the striped lionfish are full of venom. The stonefish looks like an algae-covered rock, but if something touches it, venom from one of its thirteen dorsal spines shoots out.

A golden sea horse takes cover in the Reef's sargassum weeds.

When swallowed by another fish, the pufferfish puffs itself into a round ball with spikes, causing the predator to spit it out.

The clownfish has an unusual protective symbiotic relationship with another Reef animal—the anemone. Anemones belong to the same family as coral and jellyfish. They wave their venom-filled tentacles in the water to catch food. Clownfish fool the anemones into thinking that they are

The stonefish can be mistaken for an algae-encrusted rock.

Anemones protect a clownfish from its predators.

part of the anemones' bodies. In that way, the clownfish can hide among the anemones' tentacles and be safe from predators. In return, the clownfish chase away butterflyfish and other animals that like to nibble on the tips of the anemones' tentacles.

From Smallest to Largest

Fish on the Reef come in all colors, shapes, and sizes. The smallest fish is the goby. It is only two-fifths of an inch (1 cm) long and weighs less than three-tenths of an ounce (1 gram). At the other extreme, huge cod and grouper can weigh up to 900 pounds (400 kilograms).

Some fish, such as cleaner wrasses, surgeonfish, and batfish, perform special services on the Reef. The cleaner wrasses pick parasites from the skin and teeth of larger fish. This refuse is the main diet for the wrasses. Each wrasse sets up its own cleaning station on the Reef. Other fish, such as groupers and moray eels, stop by to be cleaned. Surgeonfish and batfish are algae eaters. They keep the coral reef clear of algae. When algae grow too much, they can choke the coral and the Reef stops growing.

Some Reef fish hang out in caves or under ledges during the day and come out at night to feed. Moray eels hunt at night to catch other fish or an octopus. They also like to crush crabs with their strong teeth. Soldierfish and squirrelfish, which

Moray eels make their homes in the Reef's caves and crevices.

can be traced back more than 50 million years, also hunt their prey at night. They use their venom-filled spines as defense against predators. Scorpionfish, such as lionfish, firefish, and stonefish, also use their poisonous spines to defend themselves against predators.

The largest predatory fish in the Reef are cods, groupers, snappers, and emperors. They eat smaller fish, crabs, shrimp, sand dollars, and plankton. All of these fish are sought after by commercial and recreational fishers. However, cods and groupers less than 15 inches (38 cm) long are protected through the GBRMPA. These size limits are set in order to protect the fish so they can grow and reproduce before being caught.

OTHER MARINE LIFE

Included among the Reef's more than five thousand species of mollusks are snails, slugs, clams, oysters, mussels, octopus, and squid. Some mollusks, like clams and oysters, have shells; others, such as octopuses, squid, cuttlefish, slugs, and some snails do not. Giant clams can grow to 4 feet (1.2 m) long and to 500 pounds (227 kg). Nudibranches, which are

Nudibranches, or sea slugs, are snails without shells. There are more than three thousand species worldwide.

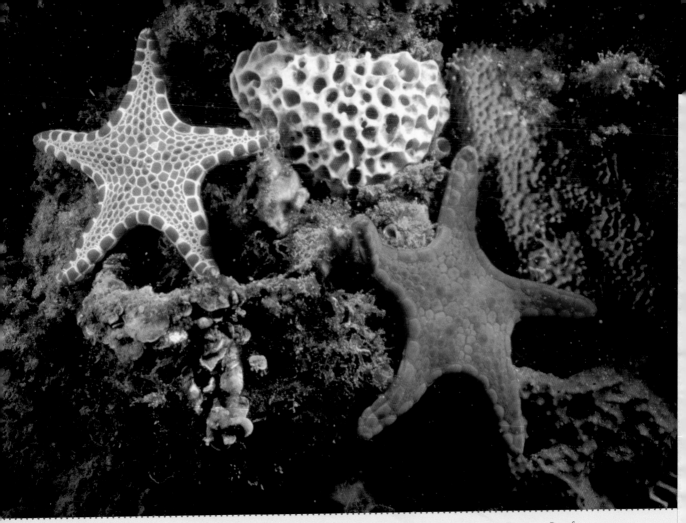

Sea stars are just one of hundreds of species that live on the Great Barrier Reef.

snails without shells, come in many colors and designs. The Spanish dancer is a type of nudibranch that seems to be wearing a swirling red and white skirt. Nudibranches prey on other animals, such as soft corals, anemones, and sponges. Sponges in many shapes and colors also grow on the Reef as well.

About eight hundred species of echinoderms live on the Reef. These animals include sea stars, sea urchins, and sea cucumbers. Sea stars are deep shades of red and blue, or can have a patterned design. They move along the coral or the sand on suction-cupped feet. Sea cucumbers pull out their food from the sand they eat. Then they excrete clean sand back to the Reef.

Several species of sharks and rays cruise the Reef's waters. Sharks serve as the Reef's main predators. They regulate the Reef's marine populations by eating sick and injured animals, as well as animals from species that are overpopulated. Hammerhead, leopard, whitetip, whale, carpet, and tiger sharks are a few of the Reef's shark species. The world's largest rays are the Reef's manta rays. They feed on small fish and plankton.

Besides dugongs, two other types of mammals also swim in the Reef's waters. Bottlenose dolphins make their way along the edges of the Reef. In winter (August to November), humpback, minke, and Byrd's whales migrate from the cold waters around Antarctica to the warm Reef waters. At the Reef, they mate and give birth to their young. As a result, whale watching has become a popular activity along the Reef.

BEYOND AND ABOVE THE REEF

Although other animals also feed on the Reef, they swim or fly back to islands where they nest. Six of the world's seven species of sea turtles live on the Reef and in

A sea turtle makes its way back to the sea after laying her eggs.

other coastal waters. These six species: the flatback, green, hawksbill, leatherback, loggerhead, and olive ridley turtles—are on the world's endangered species list. In spring and summer (November to February), the female turtles crawl up on island or cay beaches and lay their eggs in the sand. About 1,200 female turtles lay their eggs every summer. Each female turtle digs a nest in the sand, lays about one hundred eggs, and returns to the water. The eggs hatch in seven to twelve weeks. The temperature of the sand determines the turtles' sex. Eggs that hatch in warm sand produce females; those that hatch in cooler sand will be males. Then the hatchlings scurry to the lagoon. Only about one sea turtle in one thousand makes it to adulthood. Most are eaten by crabs, dogs, pigs, or shorebirds before they reach the water. Once in the water, they make a tasty snack for seabirds, fish, sharks, and crocodiles. Those turtles that do survive will return to the Reef in about twelve years because when ready to breed, turtles return to the region where they were born.

The Reef and the islands in the lagoon are also home to about 215 species of birds. These birds fall into three groups: land, shore, and sea birds. Two land birds are the pied imperial pigeon that migrates to the Reef from Papua New Guinea and the silvereye that lives on the Capricorn-Bunker Islands. The pied imperial pigeon gets its food from the Reef, but breeds and nests on the Low Isles and the Brook Islands. Seabirds of the Reef include boobies that catch flying fish in the air; cormorants; frigate birds; gulls that especially like mollusks; noddies that eat squid; petrols; prions; shearwaters; terns;

and tropic birds. Twenty-two species of these seabirds breed and nest on continental islands and coral cays. Guano—droppings—from the birds fertilizes plants on islands and coral cays.

At least thirty species of shorebirds live year-round on or migrate to cays and islands near the Reef. Several types of egrets, herons, ibises, plovers, sandpipers, and snipes are among these shorebirds. At low tide, shorebirds feed on fish left in small pools of water near shore or on other animals such as small crabs and clams. Their droppings add fertilizers to the cays and islands, thus helping plants and trees to grow.

The white-necked heron is a common bird found along the shallow waters of the Reef's cays and islands.

FOUR

"Dreaming" into the Third Millennium

From the time that the first people arrived in northeastern Australia, the Great Barrier Reef played an important part in their lives. Scientists think that the ancestors of today's Aboriginal people came to Australia between 10,000 and 50,000 years ago. Discovered remains of early people have been dated from 13,000 to 48,000 years ago. Some scientists believe that the history in Australia began as long ago as 50,000 to 70,000 years ago. Whichever period of arrival time is used, the Aboriginal people have the longest continuous culture in one area for any people on earth.

INDIGENOUS PEOPLE

The first people to live in a given area are referred to as indigenous people. They are also called native people. Aborigines, which means "the original people," make up Australia's largest group of indigenous people. Aboriginal is used as a general term for Australia's first people, in the same way that American Indian is a general term for the first people of the United States. Before Europeans settled in

Australia, as many as seven hundred separate groups, or nations, of Aborigines lived in Australia. Those groupings were similar to the various nations of American Indians, such as the Lakota, Ojibwa, and Iroquois.

Scientists believe that during the last Ice Age, the ancestors to today's Australian Aborigines crossed a land bridge from southeast Asia onto the land that is now known as Australia. At that time, the world's seas were at lower levels and more of the land, therefore, was above sea level. As the ice melted and the seas rose, other early people are believed to have arrived in Australia by using large canoes.

Australia's Aborigines, however, believe that their people have always lived in Australia. They base this belief on what is called the "Dreaming," the time when ancestor spirits created everything on earth. When the spirits completed their work, the Aborigines believe they settled in Dreaming Places such as Australia. Their Dreaming Stories tell how the Aborigines are related to the land and the sea and to the plants and animals. Because of these beliefs, the Aborigines throughout history have taken only what they needed from the land and the sea.

Before the arrival of Europeans, what is now Queensland was Australia's most heavily populated area. About 120,000 Aboriginal people from two hundred different groups made their homes there. They enjoyed a healthy and varied diet. Along the coast, they picked and gathered fruits, nuts, and vegetables that grew naturally on the land. They also waded into the lagoon and gathered many kinds

The coastal waters of Australia offered Aborigines a wealth of seafood as part of their daily diet.

of shellfish. Other Aborigines took their double-outrigger canoes beyond the offshore islands to fish and to hunt for larger sea animals near the Great Barrier Reef. Dugongs, turtles, stingrays, and sharks were especially prized catches because of their large amounts of edible meat.

The Aborigines did not just eat the meat of these animals. They made use of every possible part of the animals, in the same way that the American Indians used all parts of their deer and buffalo catches. For example, sharkskin was used as sandpaper, and shark's teeth became drills; the spine of the stingray's tail became spear

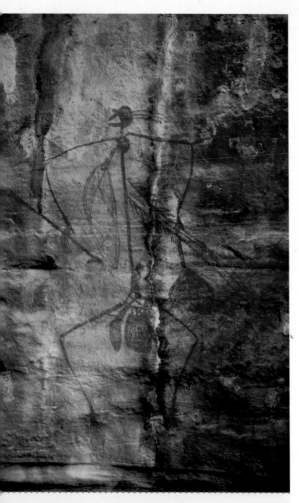
Major events were drawn on rock walls by the Aborigines. This drawing is found in Kakadu National Park.

tips. In addition, the Aborigines carved turtle shells into masks that they used in *corroborees*, ceremonial gatherings that included dances. Through these dances and accompanying songs, the Aborigines recorded important events and passed them down to the next generation. Paintings on and carvings in rock walls also recorded events. Today much of this ancient rock art is found in coastal Queensland and on nearby islands.

The Torres Strait Islanders— Melanesians who are related to the people of Papua New Guinea—make up Australia's other group of indigenous people. They have been living on islands in the Torres Strait for about ten thousand years, including islands at the northern tip of the Great Barrier Reef. Similar to the Aborigines, the Islanders also fished and hunted for food in the Reef's waters. However, they also were farmers who planted yams and taro. The Islanders engaged in trade with Aborigines and with people of Papua New Guinea. From those contacts, the Islanders' languages were influenced by the languages of the Aborigine and those from Papua New Guinea.

EUROPEAN EXPLORERS

During the 1500s and 1600s Dutch and Portuguese explorers sailed along Australia's western coast. The Dutch claimed western Australia for Holland and called that area New Holland. Some historians believe that in 1522 Portuguese explorer Cristóvão de Mendonça was the first European to see Australia's eastern coast and the area of the Great Barrier Reef. However, the first European to record his visit to the Great Barrier Reef was Portuguese explorer Manuel Godhino de Eredia in 1601. Five years later Spanish explorer Luis Vaez de Torres sailed through the strait that was later named for him.

About 150 years later, in 1768, two French ships under Louis-Antoine de Bougainville approached Australia's eastern coast. He sighted the reef that is now named for him. Bougainville Reef is about 125 miles (201 km) east of the Great Barrier Reef, almost opposite present-day Cooktown.

However, it was not until 1770 that Europeans first sailed between Australia's eastern coast and the Great Barrier Reef. In that year, English explorer Lieutenant James Cook—better known as Captain Cook—mapped the eastern coastline. He claimed eastern Australia for England and named it New South Wales. Cook also recorded the first full description of the Reef system, which he described as a labyrinth, or maze. As he sailed the HMS *Endeavour* north between the mainland, the islands, and the Reef, Cook named several sites. He named the Whitsunday Islands and Trinity Bay after special

This painting by Algernon Talmadge depicts Captain James Cook's founding of Australia.

Sundays in the Easter season. Magnetic Island was so named because the ship's compass went askew as Cook passed by. Cape Tribulation gained its name because it was near the site where the *Endeavour* hit a reef and tore a hole in its hull. Farther north is Cooktown and the Endeavour River where Cook's crew pulled the ship ashore to repair it. Two botanists—scientists who study plants—were also on board the *Endeavour.* Joseph Banks and Daniel Solander examined plants on the nearby land. These scientists also became the first Europeans to record information about the Great Barrier Reef.

At various points, Cook and his crew met with Aborigines. Cook wrote that the Aborigines seemed to be a happy and well-fed people, although the Aborigines in no way welcomed the Europeans. Other British exploratory groups came to the area of the Great Barrier Reef after the findings of Cook's voyage became known. These later groups also included scientists who studied the plants and animals of the area, as well as the water. In 1803 Matthew Flinders, a navigator and mapmaker, charted the shipping route along the southern part of the Reef out to the Coral Sea. On his maps the area of the Reef is for the first time called "The Extensive Barrier Reefs," which, over time, became known as the Great Barrier Reef. Flinders is thought to be one of the first Europeans to walk on major parts of the Reef. When Flinders left the Reef area, he did so through a passage to the Coral Sea. This passage is now called Flinders' Passage. Flinders also pushed for the entire continent to be called Australia.

In 1815 Captain Charles Jeffreys, another navigator and mapmaker, sailed the entire length of the lagoon between the mainland and the Reef. His maps were more detailed than Cook's. Those maps opened the calm waters between the

Matthew Flinders, a navigator and cartographer, surveyed the Australian coast with his small crew.

mainland and the Reef to large-scale shipping. Up until then, ships traveling along eastern Australia had to ply the rougher open waters of the Coral Sea. Although taking the inner route was safer and quicker for ships sailing between India and ports in southeastern Australia, shipwrecks continued to occur from unexpected contact with the Reef.

CHANGES TO LAND AND WATER NEAR THE REEF

In 1788 Britain established its first settlement in Australia in what is now Sydney. This settlement was a penal colony—a place for Great Britain to send its overflow of prisoners. However, in time, Australia, and particularly Queensland, became a popular destination for immigrants from England, Scotland, and Ireland to settle. In the 1850s and 1860s the immigrants cleared the land of much of its tropical forest, including mangroves. Then they planted crops, such as sugarcane, and built cattle and sheep ranches. They also established towns and cities along Queensland's coast. Townsville was founded in 1864 as a meat-processing center for nearby cattle ranches. Cairns was founded in 1876 and became a sugar-processing center. In the 1870s gold was discovered near Townsville, Port Douglas, and Cooktown, triggering a gold rush. More immigrants arrived, including some from China and areas of the South Pacific.

From the time that Australia came under British control, the British government disregarded the Aborigines' ownership of the land.

Instead, all of Australia was treated as previously unowned land. As European immigrants built farms and cities, the Aborigines were pushed farther from the coast. Many Aborigines were hired as laborers but were poorly paid and worked under harsh conditions.

By the 1890s the Reef's waters and islands near the coast had also become sources of wealth. Chinese fishers scraped the sands for *bêche-de-mer*, or sea cucumber. Dried bêche-de-mer was a delicacy in China, somewhat like a seafood version of beef jerky. Japanese pearl divers harvested

When diving for pearls, some divers wore full dive suits, while others simply held their breath.

oyster, trochus, and other shells for the coating of mother-of-pearl on the inside of the shells. These pearly shells became buttons, belt buckles, and various kinds of jewelry. Dugongs were hunted for their oil; green turtles for their meat; and hawksbill turtles for their shells, which became buckles, combs, and small dishes. People in the United States and Europe eagerly purchased these items. Guano was mined from cays and continental islands and used for fertilizer on Australian farms.

The economic development of Queensland's coastlands and of the Reef's waters brought changes to the coastal waters and to the Reef itself. Fertilizers from farms and waste from farm animals, mining, and cities ran off the land into the lagoon's water. Harvesting animals from the waters and sandy areas among the reefs upset the Reef's ecosystem and damaged the coral.

CONSERVATION EFFORTS AND SCIENTIFIC STUDIES

By the end of the 1800s the Great Barrier Reef had also become a site for tourists. In the 1880s Edmund Banfield, a Townsville journalist, wrote articles about the beauty of the Reef. He also described the Reef and nearby islands as a natural wonderland. Banfield's articles were put together into an early travel brochure that promoted the area for tourism. By the 1890s the first cruises went from Cairns to as far as Green Island. When Banfield developed health problems, he and his wife moved from Townsville to the healthier air of Dunk Island in 1897. There he became more aware that many of the Reef's animals were in danger. He wrote about the senseless hunting of pied imperial pigeons and about the loss of many dugongs through commercial overhunting by the Japanese. Through his work, Dunk Island was declared a bird sanctuary in 1905. Banfield also wrote about the need to protect and conserve the Reef itself. In 1908 he was the first person to propose that the Reef be named as a national park.

Since the early explorations of eastern Australia and the Reef in the 1700s, many British scientific expeditions have studied the Reef. One of the most famous expeditions was the Great Barrier Reef Expedition of 1928–1929 to the Low Isles. A group of coral cays form the Low Isles. This expedition added much new information about how corals grow and about the **ecology** of the Reef. The expedition's head scientist, Charles Yonge, conducted experiments to determine the relationship between coral polyps and zooxanthellae. However, he mistakenly concluded that the zooxanthellae were not a source of food for the polyps. When the expedition ended, the British scientists left a laboratory on the Low Isles and turned it over to the Australian government. This laboratory became the first Australian research station and was managed by Frank Moorhouse, the first Australian scientist of the Reef.

Scientists continued to study the Reef and how coral develops. In 1959 Thomas Goreau determined that the waste materials of the zooxanthellae are recycled by coral polyps, enabling the polyps to build their limestone shells. Goreau also linked the fact that the zooxanthellae need sunlight to the fact that living coral are only found in shallow waters. This evidence showed that zooxanthellae and polyps depend on each other. In 1983 scientists exploring the Reef at night became the first humans to document the mass spawning of coral. Before that, the occurrence of this natural phenomenon was unknown.

By the mid-1900s the growth of tourism and of new mining industries threatened the Reef. Coastal Queensland and the Reef were being used more than ever—both by residents and tourists. During the 1960s some plans were set for mining the Reef's limestone. Other plans called for oil drilling under the seabed. Resorts had been developed on Green Island, Heron Island, and the Whitsundays. By the 1970s faster boats could carry people who only wanted to spend a day on the Reef as far as 20 miles (32 km) from mainland cities. People concerned with saving the Reef's environment came forward.

In 1975 the Australian government established the Great Barrier Reef Marine Park Authority (GBRMPA) to manage the Reef's waters and marine life. The GBRMPA set up different zones in the Reef. Within each zone, certain activities, such as fishing and scuba diving, are regulated. Besides protecting nature, the GBRMPA also works to identify and protect important Aboriginal and other cultural and historic sites.

INTO THE THIRD MILLENNIUM

From the 1990s into the 2000s tourism has continued to grow. Even faster boats now carry Reef visitors 50 miles (80 km) out to Reef

waters for day trips. Reef waters also continue to provide resources. Fishing remains an important part of the economy. Recreational or sport fishers hire small fishing boats to take them out to catch coral trout, mackerel, tuna, and other fish found in Reef waters. Commercial fishers ply northern Reef waters for sea cucumber and for harvesting oyster and trochus shells. Crews on trawlers use large nets to scoop up crabs, prawns, and scallops from the continental shelf between reefs. In the process, though, many unwanted kinds of fish and animals are also scooped up and are injured or killed when tossed back. This "scooping" practice has also destroyed parts of the Reef. However, efforts have been made to limit this type of fishing. In 2004 the Australian Parliament passed a law that prohibits commercial and recreational fishing in one-third of the Reef.

Today tourism is a strong industry for the Great Barrier Reef. These visitors reef-walk off of Heron Island.

FIVE

Living Near the Reef

Although no one lives on the Reef, about 850,000 people live in the Great Barrier Reef area—on Queensland's coastline and on the continental islands and cays. From north to south, the major coastal cities are Cairns (pronounced CANS), Townsville, Mackay, Rockhampton, and Gladstone. Port Douglas and Cooktown are two good-sized towns north of Cairns. All of these cities and towns are gateways to activities on the Great Barrier Reef. The Whitsunday, Dunk, Heron, Palm, Magnetic, and Bedarra islands have small populations to support their resorts and tourist activities.

Townsville is home to the Museum of Tropical Queensland, the Reef HQ (Headquarters) Aquarium, the Australian Institute of Marine Science, James Cook University, and the Great Barrier Reef Marine Park Authority. From Townsville, dive operators run trips to a variety of nearby reefs and to famous shipwrecks, such as the

◄ *Most of the population near the Great Barrier Reef is located in cities along Australia's eastern coast. This is Brisbane.*

Yongala, the *Gothenberg*, and the *Foam*. Other shipwrecks are also in these waters, but their names are not known.

Cairns has become the main point of entry to the Reef. Thousands of foreigners arrive every day at Cairns' airport, some on direct flights from Japan. From the airport, they make their way to Reef Fleet Terminal and take a boat to any of a number of sites on the Reef.

Today, Mackay processes one-third of Australia's sugarcane crop, and the city's port is one of the world's largest sugar-loading terminals. Rockhampton calls itself the Beef Capital of Australia because of the large number of nearby cattle ranches. Gladstone has a busy port that handles exports, such as farm produce and coal. The port is also the departure point for boats heading to one of the most famous of the Reef's coral cay islands—Heron Island.

All of the coastal cities have modern urban areas with office buildings, hotels, and restaurants. Most of the towns and cities have

A Post Office on the Reef?

Yes, there is a post office on the Reef. A floating post office is on Agincourt Reef, about 45 miles (72 km) offshore from Port Douglas. Visitors have their letters or postcards stamped with a special postmark from the Great Barrier Reef.

The Gold Coast, in Queensland, is a region with high-rise buildings and miles of sandy beaches. It is a favorite destination for surfers.

preserved their early historical buildings, which now serve as tourist attractions. They have also improved their waterfronts by building beaches and walkways.

The nonindigenous population of Queensland's coastal towns and islands includes people with backgrounds that can be traced to every continent. However, people with European backgrounds—English, Scottish, Irish, German, and Italian—still make up the majority of the population. Until 1973 Australia limited non-Caucasian immigration. Since then, one-third of immigrants to coastal Queensland have come from Asian countries, including Vietnam and Laos. Many

Asians in coastal cities can trace their heritage to Chinese fishers and miners who arrived in the late 1800s.

INDIGENOUS PEOPLE TODAY

During the late 1800s and early 1900s, the British and Australian governments forced the Aborigines from their land and took away all their rights. Many children were taken from their parents and forced to learn English. As a result, Aboriginal culture and language suffered greatly. In the 1930s many Aborigines started working to regain their rights. In 1967 the Australian government recognized Aborigines as Australian citizens. Nine years later the government set up the Office of Aboriginal and Torres Strait Islander Affairs to regulate health and education issues of the indigenous people. In 1976 Australia passed a law that declared that Aborigines have land rights. In 1990 the government formed the Aboriginal and Torres Strait Islander Commission (ATSIC). Indigenous people are elected to the ATSIC to help protect their culture and improve living conditions. Finally, in 1992, Australia's highest court ruled that the Aborigines are the original, or traditional, owners of the land.

Today, from Gladstone to the Torres Strait Islands, there are more than seventy groups of Aboriginal and Torres Strait Islander people along Queensland's coast. Most of these indigenous people in the Reef area live in towns and cities or on reservations. Many continue to observe their traditional cultures. For example, Aborigines still hold corroborees at night in which they tell their stories through songs

The Aborigines continue to celebrate their culture and heritage in modern-day Australia.

and dances. The didgeridoo, a traditional Aboriginal instrument, is also still used during ceremonies. This instrument, a tree branch hollowed out by termites, is blown into to make a sound. How high or low the sound is depends on the length and width of the didgeridoo. The Tjapukai in Cairns and the KuKu-Yalanji near Port Douglas are two of the Aboriginal groups in coastal Queensland. Many visitors to the Reef experience Aboriginal culture as they learn how to play a didgeridoo or join in a corroboree at Tjapukai Aboriginal Cultural Park. Others take a Dreamtime Walk with the KuKu-Yalanji in the rain forest. In addition, visitors can view ancient Aboriginal rock paintings on Lizard and Hinchinbrook islands.

SHIPWRECKS

Whenever large numbers of people begin traveling on coastal waters, there are shipwrecks. The wreckage of more than two thousand ships lies near the Great Barrier Reef. About thirty of these wrecks have been declared of historic interest. In the far north, just east of Cape York, lie the remains of the RMS *Quetta*. In February 1890 this passenger ship sank within three minutes after hitting a huge coral mound near Adolphus Channel. Of the 292 crew and passengers, 158 made it to safety. Years later the ship's bell was recovered and now is on display at Quetta Cathedral on Thursday Island in the Torres Strait. Divers at this wreck can still see the ship's propeller and rudder, as well as remains of masts and other equipment.

Southeast of the *Quetta* divers explore what remains of the oldest known shipwreck off Australia's eastern coast. On August 29, 1791, the HMS *Pandora* sank in 108 feet (33 m) of water after hitting a reef. The ship was on its way back to England with fourteen of the mutineers from the HMS *Bounty*. The *Pandora* lost thirty-five people, four of them were mutineers. Most of the ship is now buried under sand, and what remains visible is covered with coral and algae.

One of the Great Barrier Reef's most famous shipwrecks is the *Yongala*, a passenger and cargo steamship. It sank, along with 122 crew members and passengers, during a cyclone in March 1911 on a trip from Mackay to Cairns. The remains of the ship are protected by Australia's Historic Shipwrecks Act of 1976 and by the GBRMPA. Divers are forbidden do anything to further damage the ship itself or to harm the coral that has grown on its hull. Some divers consider the *Yongala* the world's best wreck dive. They can swim among and take photos of coral trout, lionfish, damselfish, barracudas, sea snakes, groupers, and turtles, as well as hard corals, and soft corals such as fan and whip gorgonians.

Besides these ships that accidentally sank, other ships have been sunk on purpose. Coral polyps quickly attached themselves to these artificial reefs, completely covering them. Fish and other marine animals swim in and out of their new homes without knowing that the new reef was once a ship. Over time, sometimes divers cannot tell the difference either.

Dangerous areas of coastal waters are recognized when a number of ships hit the same rocks or reefs. Then, lighthouses are built. From Lady Elliot Island to the Torres Strait, twenty lighthouses stand on islands, reefs, capes, and rocks. The lighthouses on Lady Elliot Island and North Reef Island were designated as having historical importance in the Great Barrier Reef World Heritage Site. Many beacons and other navigational devices also guide ships safely between the coast and the Reef.

RECREATION ON THE REEF

Today tourism is the most important economic activity in the Great Barrier Reef area. Tourists and the money they spend on activities related to the Great Barrier Reef almost totally support Queensland's coastal cities and island resorts and provide a large amount of income for Australia and the state of Queensland. Every year, about 2 million people visit the Great Barrier Reef area and spend about $2 billion dollars while they are there. These tourists come from all over the world—the United States, Europe, Asia, South America, as well as from many other countries.

Many visitors stay at resorts on the larger islands. There they can bird-watch or guide hatchling turtles to the sea. From the islands, visitors can wade into the sea and look down at colorful fringe reefs.

More than five hundred commercial boats of various speeds and sizes carry

◄ *The reef can be dangerous for ships. Lighthouses were built to help ship captains navigate the shallow waters of the Great Barrier Reef.*

visitors to the Reef for diving, snorkeling, or other activities. Those who wish to see the coral and marine life but want to stay dry can take a ride in a glass-bottom boat or in a semi-submersible. The "semi-subs" are completely enclosed vessels with windows below the surface of the water.

More adventurous people snorkel. Wearing flippers and a mask with a breathing tube attached, they lay face down in the water and slowly swim around looking at the coral, colorful fish, and other marine life. They can take pictures with waterproof cameras.

The most adventurous visitors scuba dive on the Reef, going completely underwater as far down as they choose. All divers on the Reef

Many visitors enjoy scuba diving the Reef.

The Best Dive Sites

Although the Great Barrier Reef has hundreds of places for divers to explore underwater, the following sites appear on most top-dive-site lists.

- The wreck of the *Yongala* is surrounded by schools of barracuda, kingfish, and turrum, as well as sea snakes, bull rays, eagle rays, and a grouper as big as a Volkswagon.

- The blow hole off Lady Elliot Island was formed by waves as the sea level changed during the last Ice Age. Caves and little nooks are full of feather stars, soft corals, anemones, and manta rays.

- Heron Island Bommie has appeared in almost every movie or documentary filmed on the Great Barrier Reef. Divers can watch moray eels and parrotfish, as well as get a demonstration of how a wrasse cleans the inside of a coral trout's mouth. This site also has great examples of staghorn coral and boulder coral heads, as well as yellow-polyped turret coral.

- Cod Hole is on a ribbon reef east of Lizard Island. The highlight of this dive is feeding the potato cods—huge types of groupers.

With the abundant sea life in the waters of the Reef, it is easy to make a new friend. Though some can be dangerous.

must go through special training and show that they are certified. Seeing the many types of coral, colorful fish and anemones, and wavy sea grasses is worth the extra effort. Many divers take both daytime and nighttime dives. The kinds of marine life that are out and about during the day are completely different from the types that are active at night. To remember their adventure, most divers take pictures of the coral and other animals during their dive.

MARINE LIFE AND PEOPLE

Marine animals, like all animals, have ways to protect themselves from predators, as well as ways to attack prey. When they feel threatened, many of the Reef's inhabitants are also potentially dangerous to people. A stingray can cause injury or, though rare, death from the venom injected from the barb on its tail. The death of Steve "The Crocodile Hunter" Irwin in 2006 from a stingray's barb to the heart made headlines around the world. However, film shot of the event revealed that the stingray felt trapped. Most stingray-caused injuries occur when divers step on a ray as it is resting on the ocean floor and covered by sand. The stingray then flicks its tail up and drives its barb into whatever it perceives as a threat—in this case, the unfortunate person's foot or leg.

Venom is injected by other Reef animals as well, such as jellyfish and cone shells. The tentacles of sea jellies and box jellies are full of stinging cells that inject venom upon contact with other animals or people. Cone shells can shoot out a venom-filled harpoon into human skin. The lionfish, scorpionfish, and stonefish have venom in their spines. Some sea urchins and crown-of-thorns starfish also have venom in their spines. The result of a venom injection with can range from a skin irritation to death, if not quickly treated.

Barracuda and generally shy moray eels only attack when provoked. Both the barracuda and the moray eel have teeth that slant backward. Therefore, it is difficult to get them to release whatever they have a hold on.

Coming in contact with the coral can also result in injuries. Hard coral is sharp and will cut when handled. Some soft corals, such as fire coral, are covered with tiny hairs full of stinging cells. Touching it results in a burning itch. To protect the Reef and to safeguard themselves, divers are told not to touch or break off pieces of coral.

When diving or snorkeling in the Reef, people should follow three pieces of advice. First, they should be aware of where they are and not accidentally step or kneel on any marine animals. Second, they should only look at and take photos of the fish and other animals. Third, they should never do anything to disturb or to frighten marine life and thus provoke an attack.

SIX

Protecting the Reef

From the mid-1800s, when people began large-scale harvesting of fish and of other marine life from waters near the Reef, the Great Barrier Reef, its waters, and its marine life have been threatened. That was also the time when farms and towns began to develop on the Queensland coast. Since then, many reefs nearest the shore have almost completely broken down. Reefs farther out on the continental shelf are now in various stages of decay.

The main causes of this damage can be traced to coastal runoff, overfishing through trawling (netting and catching unwanted species while fishing), bleaching, and invasions of crown-of-thorns starfish. Cyclones and other storms also have caused damage, but, fortunately, the coral rebounds quickly from those forces of nature.

◄ *A Greenpeace diver inspects coral on the Great Barrier Reef, which is in danger of dying out due to coral bleaching, an effect of global warming.*

Human-Caused Problems

Even with regulations, damage by humans to the Reef and its waters continues. For example, coastal runoff has doubled since the GBRMPA was set up in 1975. Runoff consists of water that runs off the land into the lagoon. On its way to the lagoon, this runoff water picks up waste materials from farm animals; fertilizers used to grow better crops; pesticides and fungicides used to protect crops from insects and mold; silt or loss soil; and waste materials from household pets. When these materials reach the lagoon, they can reduce the amount of oxygen in the water and increase the amount of nutrients. This results in greater growth of algae, which causes the death of coral.

To prevent runoff from affecting the Reef, wetlands along the coast must be restored. In several areas, large swaths of mangrove trees were cleared away. Also, vegetation that naturally grows in rivers should be preserved. Mangrove trees and other plants in wetlands rivers filter out harmful materials before the water arrives at the lagoon.

Although the Australian Parliament passed a law in 2004 that prohibits fishing in one-third of the Reef, overfishing continues to be a problem. In addition, as trawler nets scoop up crabs, prawns, and scallops, the nets damage the seabed and coral. There is some good news, however. Some members of the fishing industry are starting to take responsibility for the Reef and are being more careful in how they conduct their fishing operations.

Tankers that wait off the coast of Australia can be a threat to the Reef if oil or chemicals are spilled.

Large cargo ships regularly use the shipping route between the mainland and the Reef. Their cargo ranges from oil to sugar. An oil or chemical spill would cause severe damage to the Reef and its marine life. Fortunately, so far, there has not been a major oil spill near the Great Barrier Reef. However, the daily release of waste products and **ballast** water from ships pollutes the water. In addition, ballast water introduces alien species of marine life—species that come from other parts of the world—to the Reef.

CROWN-OF-THORNS STARFISH

Crown-of-thorns starfish have probably lived on the Reef for more than ten thousand years. Polyps from hard corals are part of the natural diet of crown-of-thorns. In the past, the crown-of-thorns acted as a form of coral population control. By eating faster-growing hard coral, such as staghorn and plate coral, the crown-of-thorns made room for slower-growing corals to form colonies on the Reef. In the past, this eating pattern has gone through stages that lasted from one to fifteen years.

Since the 1960s, however, the crown-of-thorns have been eating polyps more often and for longer periods of time.

Crown-of-thorns starfish have become a threat to ▶▶ *the Reef's coral. They can consume coral (as shown here) faster than the coral can reproduce.*

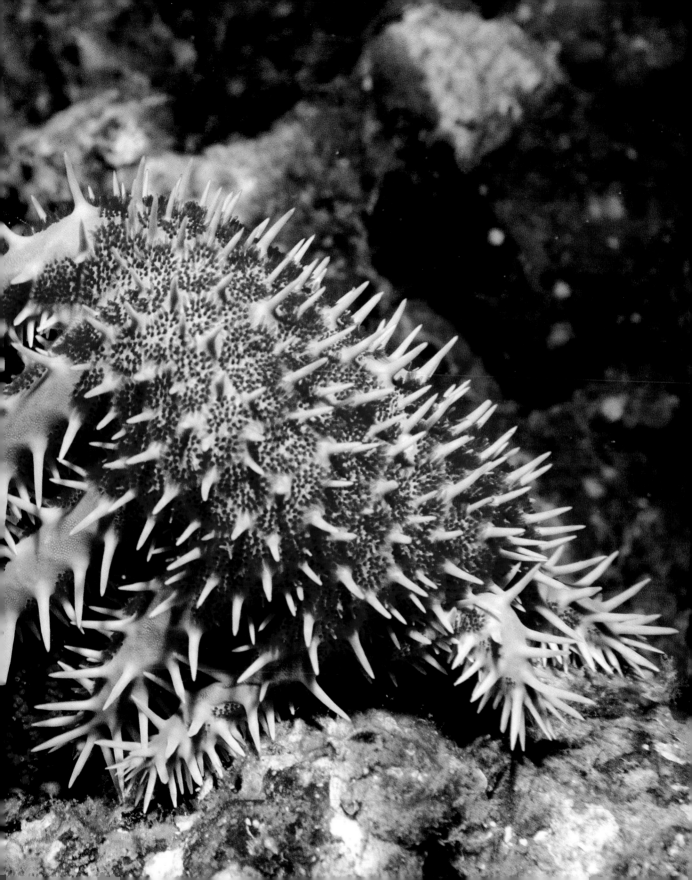

A Great Barrier Reef Marine Park employee photographs bleached coral in an area of the Reef in 2006.

One adult crown-of-thorns starfish can eat 7 square yards (6 sq. m) of living reef in one year. Scientists consider more than thirty of these starfish present in 2.5 acres (1 hectare) of Reef to be an outbreak. When this happens, the crown-of-thorns eat the coral faster than the coral can grow and reproduce. In this way, the crown-of-thorns make it harder and harder for the coral reef to recover.

CORAL BLEACHING

In coral bleaching, large numbers of coral turn white and then die. Bleaching occurs when the water temperatures are too warm. Some scientists think that coral bleaching is related to the El Niño effect. This natural weather phenomenon causes an unusual increase in the temperature of surface water. Others believe it is an effect of human-caused global warming. Whatever the reason, the zooxanthellae that live inside coral polyps cannot live in overly warm waters. When they die, so do the polyps.

Mass coral bleaching events—when large numbers of coral turn white and die at the same time—have recently occurred in the summers of 1998, 2002, and 2006. Scientists are worried that this could become an annual event. If that happens, they predict that the Great Barrier Reef could become extinct between 2025 and 2030. One report stated that during the most recent coral bleaching, about 55 percent of the Reef system was damaged.

Scientists have found that the coral of the Great Barrier Reef has died off many times in the past. The good news is that within one hundred years of those events, coral polyps repopulated the Reef. The last time that the living Reef died was about 1,500 years ago. The situation is much different today than in the ancient past, however. Now, about one million people live near the Reef with another

2 million visiting it every year. Whether a dead reef could bounce back as quickly under such an impact, or at all, is a great unknown.

The Aborigines believe that life forms one great web and that man is only a strand of that web. Humans are tightly bound with the land, water, and all of nature, including the Great Barrier Reef. At this time in the twenty-first century in the third millennium, all members of the human family should be concerned about protecting the seventh natural wonder of the world—the Great Barrier Reef.

The Great Barrier Reef is one of the world's most spectacular natural wonders. With the help of protection plans, the Reef and its wildlife can continue to be one of the world's most important natural wonders.

Glossary

algae small plants with no roots or stems that grow in water, providing food for fish and other marine animals

ballast water that a ship takes on when cargo is unloaded and that a ship releases when cargo is loaded; keeps the ship balanced and stable but can contain plant or animal life that may be harmful when released in another body of water

barrier reef a coral reef that runs parallel to a shoreline, protecting the shoreline from rough ocean waves and creating a lagoon between itself and the land; also called a ribbon or outer reef

cay a low island formed by buildup of ground-up coral

continental shelf a shallow underwater area of land that forms a coastal border for a continent, ending in a steep slope to the deep ocean floor

coral a polyp or colony of polyps, as well as the hardened limestone deposited by them

ecology the study of the relationship among plants, animals, humans, and their environment

ecosystem a community of plants, animals, and humans interacting with their natural environment

fringe reef a coral reef that forms a border along a shoreline

lagoon   shallow, calm water separated from the sea by a narrow strip of land, a chain of islands, or a barrier reef

platform reef   a round or oval isolated patch of reef between the mainland and larger parts of a barrier reef

polyp   a tiny animal that forms coral reefs

species   a group of plants or animals with many of the same characteristics

symbiotic relationship   a relationship between two living things that is beneficial to both

zooplankton   a microscopic animal that floats in water and is eaten by coral polyps and other sea animals

zooxanthellae   the species of algae that lives inside coral polyps, providing them with food

Fast Facts

Name: Great Barrier Reef

Other names: Murgur, in the Wulguru Aborigine language

Date of completion: About eight thousand years ago, but actually an ongoing process

Coral Sea

Location: Coral Sea of the South Pacific Ocean, along the northeastern coast of Australia

Surface area: 134,115 square miles (348,700 sq. km) [Great Barrier Reef Marine Park]; 752,000 square miles (1.9 million sq. km) [Great Barrier Reef Province]

Greatest distance north to south: 1,428 miles (2,300 km)

Greatest distance east to west: 124 miles (200 km)

Borders: To the east, the Coral Sea; to the south, Lady Elliot Island; to the west, the Torres Strait and the lagoon waters that separate it from the land of Queensland, Australia; to the north, Booby Island in the Torres Strait (the Gulf of Papua near Papua New Guinea)

Highest elevation: Sea level

Lowest elevation: 197 feet (60 m) below sea level

Average water temperatures: 66 °F (19 °C) in July (winter); 82 °F (28 °C) in February (summer)

Population of nearby land: 850,000

Population of largest nearby metropolitan areas (2006 est.):

Townsville, Queensland   153,631
Cairns, Queensland   127,856
Mackay, Queensland   73,091
Rockhampton, Queensland   70,128
Gladstone, Queensland   43,507

Major islands and cays: Dunk Island, Great Keppel Island, Heron Island, Hinchinbrook Island, Lady Elliot Island, Lizard Island, Magnetic Island, Whitsunday Islands

Famous dive and snorkel sites: Clam Gardens, Cod Hole, Fitzroy Reef Lagoon, Lady Elliot Island, Osprey Reef, Pixie's Pinnacle

Economy: Boating, fishing, shipping, tourism

Famous people:

Edmund Banfield (1852–1923), English journalist and naturalist who settled in Townsville, Queensland, and later moved to Dunk Island; wrote about the beauty of the Great Barrier Reef and became a pioneer of the movement to preserve the Reef; suggested in 1908 to preserve the Reef within a national park.

James Cook, known as Captain Cook (1728–1779), as commander of HMS *Endeavour* (1770), he became the first European to explore the eastern coast of Australia and to navigate between the coastline and what would become known as the Great Barrier Reef; named many sites along the coast, including Whitsunday Islands, Trinity Bay, Cape Tribulation; Cooktown is named after him.

James Cook

Robert Fitzroy (1805–1865), commander of HMS *Beagle* on voyage (1831–1836) with Charles Darwin; explored the eastern coast of Australia; Fitzroy Island is named after him.

Matthew Flinders (1774–1814), English explorer and surveyor who sailed Australia's coastline and named the Great Barrier Reef.

Steve "The Crocodile Hunter" Irwin (1962–2006), Australian wildlife expert, conservationist, and television personality from southeastern Queensland; died while filming the documentary *Ocean's Deadliest* in the Great Barrier Reef near Port Douglas when he and a cameraman accidentally boxed in a stingray; to protect itself, the ray attacked with its venomous barbed tail, stabbing Irwin in the heart.

Judith Wright (1915–2000), Australian poet, environmentalist, and worker for Aboriginal land rights; fought to protect the ecology of the Great Barrier Reef (1960s and 1970s) from oil drilling and mining, which she wrote about in her book *The Coral Battleground* (1977).

Famous shipwrecks:

HMS *Pandora*, 1791
RMS *Quetta*, 1890
SS *Yongala*, 1911

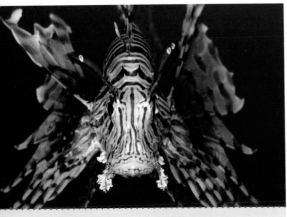

Lionfish

Animals: 400 species of corals—brain, bush fan, finger, fire, mushroom, pineapple, scroll, staghorn, star, whip; 1,500 kinds of fish—batfish, blennies, butterflyfish, clownfish, cod, emperors, firefish, gobies, grouper, lionfish, parrotfish, pufferfish, sea horses, snappers, stonefish, surgeon, wrasse; 5,000 species of mollusks—clams, cuttlefish, mussels, octopuses, oysters, slugs, snails, squid;

Egret

800 species of echinoderms—sea cucumbers, sea urchins, starfish; more than 30 species of mammals—dolphins, dugongs, whales; other animals—anemones, jellyfish, rays, sea snakes, sharks, sponges, worms; 6 species of turtles—flatback, green, hawksbill, leatherhead, loggerhead, olive ridley; 215 species of birds—boobies, cormorants, egrets, frigate birds, gulls, ibises, noddies, petrols, pied imperial pigeons, plovers, prions, sandpipers, shearwaters, silvereye, snipes, terns, tropic birds

Plants: *Halimeda*, *Lithothamnion*, and *Porolithon* algae; zooxanthellae algae; sea grasses; eucalyptus and mangrove trees

Greatest threats: Bleaching, crown-of-thorns starfish, global warming, overfishing, pollution from runoff and from shipping industry

Find Out More

BOOKS

Collard, Sneed B. *One Night in the Coral Sea*. Watertown, MA: Charlesbridge Publishing, 2005.

Myline, Lee. *Australia's Great Barrier Reef*. Frommer's Portable, 4th edition. Hoboken, NJ: Wiley Publishing, 2007.

Parks, Peggy. *The Great Barrier Reef* (Wonders of the World series). Farmington Hills, MI: Kidhaven Press, 2005.

Zell, Len. *Great Barrier Reef: Diving and Snorkeling*. Footscray, Victoria, Australia: Lonely Planet Publications, 2006.

DVDS

Australia the Beautiful. Reader's Digest Video and Television, Chicago, 2004.

Imax Presents: The Great Barrier Reef. Vista Point Entertainment, 2006.

WEB SITES

Diving Cairns

www.divingcairns.com

Information is mainly about diving and snorkeling, dive sites, and diving instructions but also includes pages with information about the Reef and its marine life.

The Great Barrier Reef

www.greatbarrierreef.org

Many pages with information about the history, environment, marine life, mainland cities, and islands of the Reef.

Great Barrier Reef Marine Park Authority

www.gbrmpa.gov.au

Official Web site of this national marine park; includes information about how the park is zoned, the uses of each zone, and ways to protect the Reef.

Great Barrier Reef Visitors Bureau

www.greatbarrierreef.aus.net

Besides information about weather, maps, and currency, this Web site has pages about tours and attractions in the main towns and islands near the Reef.

reefED—educate to keep it great

www.reefed.edu.au

Includes pages on Reef animals and plants, indigenous peoples, and how water quality affects the Reef, as well as a great section just for students.

Index

Page numbers in **boldface** are illustrations and charts.

ABOUT THE AUTHOR

Patricia K. Kummer has a B.A. degree in history from the College of St. Catherine in St. Paul, Minnesota, and an M.A. degree in history from Marquette University in Milwaukee, Wisconsin. She has contributed chapters to several American and world history textbooks and has written more than sixty books about states, countries, inventions, and other topics. Books she has written for Marshall Cavendish include the revised editions of *Minnesota* and *Mississippi* in the Celebrate the States series and *The Great Lakes* in the Nature's Wonders series.

Ms. Kummer lives with her husband in Lisle, Illinois, a suburb of Chicago. They enjoy spending time with their grown children and young granddaughters, as well as traveling.